BAD GUYS

OUTLAWS

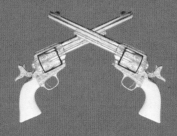

BAD GUYS

OUTLAWS

by Gary L. Blackwood

BENCHMARK BOOKS

MARSHALL CAVENDISH
NEW YORK

Benchmark Books
Marshall Cavendish Corporation
99 White Plains Road
Tarrytown, New York 10591-9001
Website: www.marshallcavendish.com

© Marshall Cavendish Corporation 2002

Library of Congress Cataloging-in-Publication Data

Blackwood, Gary L.
Outlaws / by Gary L. Blackwood
p.cm.—(Bad guys ; 2)
Includes bibliographical references (p.) and index.
ISBN 0-7614-1015-5 (lib. bdg.)
1. Outlaws—United States—History—19th century—Juvenile literature. 2. Outlaws—United States—Biography—Juvenile literature. [1. Robbers and outlaws.] I. Title.

HV6446.B56 2001   364.15'52'0973—dc21   00-057161

Book Design by Gysela Pacheco

Picture research by Linda Sykes Picture Research, Hilton Head SC

Front Cover: Amon Carter Museum, Fort Worth TX; page 1:Buffalo Bill Historical Center, Cody, WY, Gift of Lillian Burch Thomson; pages 2, 34 48: Stock Montage, Inc.; pages 7, 16, 26, 32: © Corbis; pages 9, 23, 50, 54, 60: The Granger Collection; page10: California History Section/ California State Library; page 13: Photograph provided by Swann Galleries with permission of R. G. McCubbin Collection; pages 18, 38: Brown Brothers; pages 21, 22: Minnesota Historical Society; pages 25, 44, 56: Bettmann/ Corbis; page 28: Kansas State Historical Society; page 29: Wittliff Gallery of Southwestern and Mexican Photography/ Southwest Texas State University; page 37: North Wind Pictures; page 41: Courtesy of Wells Fargo; page 59: State Historical Society of Missouri

Printed in Italy

1 3 5 6 4 2

Contents

Introduction

Historians generally agree that the Wild West was not nearly as wild as movies and Western novels portray it. Gunfights were not an everyday event in most frontier towns, and only a handful of the most notorious gunmen could claim a death toll in the double digits.

Yet there's no denying that the Old West was a dangerous place. In the final three decades of the nineteenth century, an estimated 20,000 Westerners died of "lead poisoning"—gunshot wounds, in other words.

That's hardly surprising, considering what sorts of people were attracted to the West. They were, by and large, the ones who couldn't fit in back in the "civilized" East. Many were in trouble with the law in their home states. Some were impetuous boys not yet out of their teens. Others were veterans of the Civil War, to whom fighting was second nature.

Most were looking for a less confining and less conventional way of life. Unfortunately, one of the few professions to offer that sort of freedom, and a decent income as well, was outlawry.

In our own century, two very different images of the Western outlaw have developed. One portrays him, in the words of historian Joseph Henry Jackson, as "a

In the Wild West, firearms and firewater could be a deadly combination. Under the influence of alcohol, men who were ordinarily reasonable and law-abiding often turned nasty, even violent.

daring, gallant, rip-snorting sort of fellow who has done no more than take from society what was rightfully his." The other, darker image is of a homicidal maniac with no compassion and no conscience.

This ambivalent attitude toward outlaws isn't just a modern phenomenon. In their own time they were romanticized by half the public, who saw them as mis-understood heroes. The other half denounced them as deranged, degraded, and downright despicable.

The truth, as you'll see from the stories that follow, was nearly always somewhere in between.

One
The Mexican Bandit

The Wild West era is usually thought of as beginning around 1865, just after the Civil War. But in reality it got under way some fifteen years earlier, when a gold strike at Sutter's Mill brought fortune seekers flooding into California.

Since California had long been part of Mexico, many of the early miners were Hispanics. New arrivals from "the States," resentful of the fact that so many claims were held by these "foreigners," pressured the California legislature into passing the Foreign Miners Tax Law. It required miners who were not "native or natural-born citizens of the United States" to obtain a costly license and renew it every thirty days. Those who protested were driven off, whipped, or even hanged. Robbed of their rights, some Mexican-American miners turned to robbery themselves, preying on ranchers, settlers, and miners, and shooting anyone who stood in their way.

Joaquin Murieta was destined to become the most celebrated of these bandits, not because of anything he actually did, but because of a wildly popular—and almost wholly fictitious—account of his career. Murieta was in fact only one of at least five outlaws named Joaquin. In 1853 a company of rangers was formed to capture any or

The 1849 gold rush attracted a flood of fortune seekers from all over the world, turning California towns like San Francisco into bustling trade centers.

all of "the five Joaquins." They returned with the head of an unidentified bandit chief. Since the rangers couldn't collect the thousand-dollar reward for an unnamed head, they arbitrarily dubbed it the head of Joaquin Murieta.

For years the head, preserved in alcohol, was exhibited in saloons and museums around the region. Legend has it that the ranger responsible for lopping it off was haunted by Joaquin's ghost, demanding the return of his head. In 1854 journalist John Rollin Ridge published a "biography" titled *The Life and Adventures of Joaquin Murieta*. The book transformed Murieta into a larger-than-life folk hero, a Mexican Robin Hood.

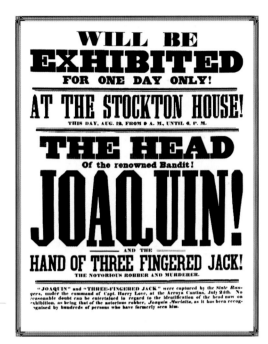

Rangers who brought in "the head of Murieta" also killed a bandit known as Three Fingered Jack and lopped off the hand with the missing digits. As this poster indicates, the two trophies were sometimes displayed together.

Well before Ridge's book appeared, a boy named Tiburcio Vasquez, inspired by tales of the five Joaquins, started a criminal career that would span two decades and rival the exploits of the mythical Murieta.

Born in 1837 in Monterey, Tiburcio attended school long enough to become adept at reading, writing, and arithmetic. "As I grew up to manhood," he later told a newspaper reporter, "I was in the habit of attending balls and parties . . . into which the [Anglo] Americans . . . would force themselves and force the native-born men aside, monopolizing the dance and the women."

A growing "spirit of hatred and revenge" drove the fifteen-year-old into a series of fights, including one in which a police constable was fatally stabbed. Knowing he could expect no justice from *gringo* authorities, Tiburcio went into hiding. When things calmed down he returned home, only to find police waiting for him. After a brief gunfight, he escaped, determined now to "live off the world."

According to tradition, Vasquez joined Joaquin Murieta's gang—a doubtful claim, since the five Joaquins were active only a few more months. He did fall in with a thief named Garcia, who taught him the fine points of cattle rustling. In August 1855, still only twenty years old, Vasquez was captured and sentenced to five years in San Quentin.

After his release he "endeavored to lead a peaceful and honest life"—if becoming a gambler can be considered honest. Then the robbery and murder of an Italian butcher led the sheriff to summon Vasquez—not as a suspect, but as an interpreter at the inquest. When Vasquez disappeared the following day, authorities concluded that he had been involved in the murder.

For a year or so Vasquez stayed on the move, stealing a few horses here and some cattle there—and also stealing away a rancher's daughter. One version of the story has the irate father pursuing Vasquez, shooting him in the arm (wounding his daughter in the process), and carrying the girl back home.

The rancher's daughter was not the first woman to fall prey to Vasquez's charms, or the last. After a friend let the outlaw hide out in his home, Vasquez showed his gratitude by abducting the man's young wife. Later he won the affection of the wife of another bandit, who got his revenge by turning himself in and then testifying against his fellow thieves.

In 1865 Vasquez was arrested for rustling cattle, and

spent another three years behind bars. No sooner was he discharged than he gathered together a band of outlaws and embarked on a four-year crime spree that made him the most wanted man in the state of California.

The gang's first target was a stagecoach. After the passengers were relieved of their valuables, they were ordered to lie on the ground while their wrists and ankles were tightly bound—a method that became Vasquez's trademark. A posse pursued the gang, and one lawman shot Vasquez in the chest. The bandit managed to ride sixty miles into the hills, where he recovered in the care of friends.

He had little trouble finding sympathy and support among Mexican Americans, who saw him as a victim of injustice, wreaking vengeance on the *gringos.* They recounted stories that demonstrated Vasquez's decency and generosity—and that sounded suspiciously similar to tales told about countless other outlaws back to the time of Robin Hood.

Vasquez seriously undermined his reputation for gallantry during a raid on a general store in the California town of Tres Pinos. Everything went smoothly at first. While Vasquez stood guard, his men robbed the clerk and the customers, and trussed them up in the usual fashion. Then the trouble began.

A Portuguese sheepherder approached the store. When he ignored a command to halt, Vasquez shot him down. Two teamsters outside the store tried to run off, but the outlaw felled one with a blow to the head and shot the other through the heart. Another bystander

According to a reporter who interviewed Tiburcio Vasquez shortly before his execution, the outlaw cautioned mothers to keep their children away from "degrading influence" and warned his fellow bandits to mend their ways.

dived into a nearby hotel and slammed the door. Vasquez fired through the door, killing a man inside. A small boy who ran into the street was knocked unconscious by one of Vasquez's men.

Public outrage over the "Tres Pinos Massacre" spurred law enforcement agencies into action. After the gang tied up thirty-five citizens of Kingston and plundered two stores and a hotel, the governor posted a reward of $8,000 for Vasquez's arrest.

For a time the gang laid low. The San Francisco *Chronicle* printed a rumor that Vasquez, dressed in women's clothing, had caught a steamer for Mexico. But then he and his men turned up at a sheep ranch and ordered the owner to hand over the $10,000 he had just received from selling his stock. The rancher protested that he had used the money to buy land. Vasquez demanded to see his books and receipts. Satisfied that the man had told the truth, the outlaw proceeded to ask him for a loan.

When the rancher sent his nephew to fetch the money from the bank, the boy alerted the authorities. By the time lawmen reached the ranch, the outlaws had fled. The posse, accompanied by a newspaper reporter, trailed the bandits to their hideout and surrounded it. Vasquez leaped from a window, but was brought down by a blast from the reporter's shotgun.

At the outlaw's trial, the courtroom, according to one newspaper's account, was "filled with ladies representing the elite and respectability of the city." Vasquez was swiftly found guilty. The judge sentenced him to hang, calling his life "one unbroken record of lawlessness and outrage, a career of pillage and murder."

The sheriff's office sent out formal, printed invitations to the execution. On the morning he was to hang, Vasquez was asked whether he believed in life after death. "I hope so," he replied, "for in that case tomorrow I will see all my old sweethearts together!"

Two

The Ex-Guerrilla

When the Civil War broke out, men with criminal tendencies suddenly found they could rob and kill all they wanted, provided their victims could be considered "the enemy." But some went on committing atrocities long after the war was officially over. Many were former Confederate soldiers or sympathizers. Though they were motivated by profit, not patriotism, they were hailed as heroes by embittered fellow Southerners.

The best known of these soldiers-turned-outlaws was Jesse James. Though he had waged war on the Yankees for only a little over a year, his battle against law and order would go on for more than fifteen years and make him, in the words of one newspaper reporter, "the most renowned murderer and robber of his age."

Jesse liked to give the impression that he was merely getting revenge for all the injustices the South had suffered. That was, of course, mainly just an excuse. Still, Jesse did have plenty of reasons to hold a grudge against the North.

In 1847, the year Jesse was born, Missouri was in the very center of the storm that raged over the problem of slavery. By 1856 gangs of anti-slavery "Jayhawkers" from Kansas—including the notorious John Brown—

In this photo a teenaged Jesse James assumes a soldierlike scowl. But in person Jesse looked deceptively boyish and innocent—partly due to the fact, as a result of a childhood eye affliction, he batted his eyelashes continually.

were raiding, and often killing, slave-owning Missouri farmers. Jesse and his friends played a game they called Old John Brown, in which they pretended to trounce the abolitionist and chase him back across the border.

After war was declared in 1861, Jesse's brother Frank enlisted in a troop of irregulars, or guerrillas, fighting for the Confederate cause. Though Jesse was too young to join the band, he served as a messenger and lookout. In the summer of 1863 Union troops descended on the family's farm near Kearny, looking for information about the guerrillas. When Jesse refused to reveal anything, the Yankees horsewhipped him. Then they repeatedly hanged his stepfather by the neck in an attempt to make him talk. Though the stepfather survived the ordeal, he lost his mind.

That fall Jesse joined a group of irregulars led by "Bloody Bill" Anderson. It's hard to imagine him fitting in with such a rough bunch. Jesse was vain about his looks, and didn't drink or swear. Even when he accidentally shot the end off his left middle finger, the worst curse he could manage was "Dingus!" That became his nickname.

His daring and coolness under fire earned him the respect of his comrades. "For a beardless boy of seventeen," said one man, "he is the most fearless fighter in the command." Thanks to his smooth cheeks and slight build, he once visited a local brothel disguised as a girl and arranged the ambush of a dozen Union soldiers.

A few days after the South surrendered in April 1865, Jesse and six other guerrillas rode into Lexington,

Missouri, to give themselves up. Instead they were attacked by Union cavalry, and Jesse was shot in the right lung. It seemed certain that he would die, but when he was taken to his uncle's house in Kansas City and placed under the care of his pretty cousin Zerelda Mimms, he gradually recuperated—and, not so gradually, fell in love.

In February 1866, a band of outlaws robbed a bank in Liberty, Missouri, of over $60,000. The holdup caused a sensation, partly because a local college student was

Even the worst outlaws had some redeeming qualities. Jesse James (at right in this photo) and his brother Frank were devoted to their mother and regularly returned home to visit her between holdups.

shot, partly because it was the first time a bank had been robbed in broad daylight during peacetime.

Six of the robbers were identified as guerrillas who had ridden with Frank James. It's uncertain whether or not Frank and Jesse were involved. Jesse's mother swore they weren't, and pointed out that Jesse still hadn't recovered from his wound. But three years later she was caught trying to pay off a loan with revenue stamps taken in the Liberty holdup.

Without the benefit of photographs or fingerprints, it was hard for law officers to pin anything on the James brothers. But during a bank holdup in Gallatin, Missouri, one of the robbers left behind a horse that, according to the Kansas City *Times,* "was identified as belonging to a young man named James. . . . The man with him was his brother, and both are very desperate and determined men."

Even though the gang had killed half a dozen town-folk, lawmen, and bank tellers, the general public wasn't particularly upset over the robberies; in fact many people were delighted. Banks were not popular institutions. They charged high interest rates on loans, and foreclosed on poor farmers who couldn't make mortgage payments.

Railroads weren't any more popular. They were mostly owned by Yankees, and often charged exorbitant shipping rates, so Southerners didn't mind much when Jesse and his men moved on to holding up trains. Apparently Jesse's cousin Zee didn't object, either. She married him in 1874, and in time they had two children, Jesse Edwards and Mary.

The banks and railroads weren't so forgiving. They hired the famous Pinkerton detective agency to track down the James brothers. In January 1875, detectives surrounded the family farm and, hoping to flush out Frank and Jesse, tossed a blazing iron ball through a window. The device exploded, killing Jesse's eight-year-old half brother and mangling his mother's forearm so badly that it had to be amputated.

Pinkerton officials claimed that the object was only a flare, but recently uncovered records indicate that it was a bomb. The incident worked up even more public sympathy for the Jameses, and a campaign began to obtain a pardon for them.

In September the gang raided a bank in Northfield, Minnesota. According to gang member Cole Younger, they hoped to make one big haul and then retire. The plan failed miserably. The outlaws were routed by the townspeople, who shot two of them. A posse killed another, and captured the three Younger brothers. Only the James boys escaped.

Jesse decided to lie low for a while, partly for health reasons—his old chest wound had opened up. This, plus the news that his sister Susan planned to marry a man he despised, threw him into a deep depression. He deliberately took an overdose of morphine, a drug he used regularly as a painkiller. Frank fetched a doctor, who managed to keep Jesse awake and active by convincing him that "persons who were very obnoxious to him were coming and it was very necessary to escape or defend to the death."

In most of their raids, the James gang had encountered little resistance, so when the citizens of Northfield, Minnesota, opened fire on them, they were unprepared.

When Jesse recovered, he took his wife and children to Tennessee where for five years he successfully posed as a respectable farmer and trader. Then in 1881 two trains were robbed near Kansas City, Missouri. Jesse's mother declared that it couldn't have been her boys, because they were both dead. But it was clear that Jesse had returned to what he called "the business." Using the alias Thomas Howard, he was now living in St. Joseph, Missouri.

The new governor of Missouri, upset over its growing reputation as "the bandit state," offered a reward of $5,000 for each of the James boys. In April 1882, two young recruits to the gang, Bob and Charlie Ford, made

It was never proven conclusively that the James boys were involved in the Northfield raid. But the Younger brothers—who were taken alive—and the three dead outlaws were all regular members of the James gang. The three men pictured at the top of this souvenir card are townspeople who were killed in the fray.

Jesse James's colorful career and his dramatic death—depicted here in a 1927 illustration—have inspired dozens of dime novels, a stage play, a number of motion pictures (including one that starred Jesse's son) and a well-known folk song, "The Ballad of Jesse James."

a bid to collect it. As the brothers sat in Jesse's house planning a robbery, Jesse unexpectedly removed his gun belt. Then, according to Charlie Ford, he "went to brush off some pictures and when he turned his back I gave my brother the wink and we both pulled our pistols, but he, my brother, was the quickest and fired first . . . I saw his shot was a death shot."

How could a fugitive who had survived so long by using his wits be so easily brought down? Some scholars think that Jesse was simply weary of running and let himself be shot, feeling that his family would be better off without him. But, despite all the money Jesse had stolen over the years, Zee and the children were left almost penniless and were forced to auction off all their household goods.

Three

The Gunman

After the Civil War the Southern states abolished slavery and declared their loyalty to the Union. But they balked at being told how to govern themselves. To bring the South into line, Congress passed a series of Reconstruction Acts that, among other things, recognized the civil rights of blacks and denied former Confederate leaders the right to vote. In many states transplanted Northerners, known as carpetbaggers, gained control of the government. Some used their position as a way of getting rich.

Texas was hit especially hard by Reconstruction. It had become a magnet for men anxious to escape government authority, including thousands of Southerners who refused to admit defeat. Resentful at being invaded by Reconstructionists, they retaliated violently, robbing and murdering Union supporters.

John Wesley Hardin, perhaps the West's most notorious gunman, blamed the chaos of the Reconstruction era for his own lawless behavior. But in fact it was mostly the result of two other factors: Hardin's nasty temper and his dislike of Mexicans and African Americans.

Hardin was born in Bonham, Texas, in 1853. Though his father, a preacher, named him after the founder of

In this early photo, a fashionably dressed John Wesley Hardin looks every inch a gentleman. In later years, he wore a less conventional piece of clothing—a vest with pockets designed to conceal a pair of short-barreled guns.

the Methodist church, young Wes was no saint. At the tender age of eleven he got into a knife fight with another boy. At fifteen he quarreled with a black farmhand. The man attacked him with a stick and Wes, who was already beginning to pack a pistol, shot him dead. Then, Hardin recalled, "I became a fugitive not from justice . . . but from the injustice and misrule of the people who had subjugated the South." When three state militiamen—two of them black—came after him, he ambushed them and killed all three. Sympathetic neighbors buried the bodies so well that they were never found.

Despite his criminal record, Wes was hired as a schoolteacher. He quit after only three months and took up the carefree life of a cowboy, spending his spare time in saloons and at the racetrack. His skill at a form of poker called seven-up earned him the nickname Little Seven-Up. A man who had lost a good deal of money to Wes took a shot at him, but missed. Wes didn't.

By the time he was eighteen, Hardin had several

Gambling, like alcohol, was often an excuse for violence. One of John Wesley Hardin's shootouts was sparked by a dispute over a card game.

more killings to his credit, and a reputation as one of the most dangerous men in Texas. In Abilene he met up with a man whose reputation was far more widespread—Wild Bill Hickok, the city's marshal. As Hardin remembered it, Hickok ordered him to hand over his guns, "but while he was reaching for them I reversed them and whirled them over on him"—a move known as the "road agent's spin."

Hickok was impressed. "You are the gamest and quickest boy I ever saw," he supposedly said. "Let us compromise this matter and I will be your friend."

It was a short-lived friendship. Hardin proceeded to shoot a fellow poker player, an intruder, and—according to legend, anyway—a man in an adjoining hotel room whose snoring was keeping him awake. Not eager to tangle with Hickok again, he made a hasty departure and returned to Gonzales, Texas, where he had met and fallen in love with a local girl named Jane Bowen. They married in March 1872 and had three children. For a time Hardin tried to live peacefully. But another quarrel ended in the usual fashion, and he was on the run again.

The gunman celebrated his twenty-first birthday by shooting it out with Charles Webb, a deputy sheriff who had vowed to arrest Hardin "or die in the attempt." Webb had to settle for his second choice. With a $4,000 reward on his head, Hardin took his family to Alabama, then Florida. Under the name J. H. Swain, he ran a saloon and a logging business, until Texas Rangers learned where he was.

As Hardin was boarding a train, Rangers surrounded him. He tried to shoot his way free, but his pistol caught

Wild Bill Hickok's notoriety was based largely on an exaggerated account of his exploits that appeared in Harper's *magazine. Though his celebrated skill with a gun inspired fear in many lawbreakers, it also made him a target for younger gunfighters seeking to enhance their own reputations.*

in his suspenders and he was taken without firing a shot. Hardin was convicted of murdering Charles Webb and sentenced to twenty-five years in prison.

At first he was bitter and rebellious. He organized a mass escape attempt, and nearly succeeded in capturing the prison armory. As punishment, he was severely beaten and spent two months in solitary confinement. Later, when he refused to work, guards threw him into a tank that could be kept from filling with water only by constant pumping. Hardin stood stubbornly with the water closing over him until the guards dragged him out, nearly drowned.

Eventually his attitude mellowed. He joined the prison debating society, taught Sunday school, and studied religion, mathematics, and law. He wrote loving letters to his wife, whose health was failing,

Jane Hardin had no illusions about what sort of man her husband was or what sort of life he lived, yet she remained loyal to him until her death.

promising that when he was free he would do his best to "cheer her and make her happy."

In 1894, having served fifteen years of his sentence, he was pardoned and released—too late to keep his promise to Jane. She had died a year and a half earlier. The forty-one-year-old former outlaw found everything changed. There were no more cattle drives and no more buffalo. The Indians were confined to reservations. All his old friends and enemies were dead.

Hardin seemed to have changed, too. An acquaintance called him "a thoroughly reformed gentleman." He began work on an autobiography, in which he claimed to have killed thirty-five men. (That was probably an exaggeration; the confirmed total is closer to a dozen.) He set up a law practice in El Paso, married a much younger woman, and avoided saloons, racetracks, and gambling halls.

But then his wife abruptly left him, and things began to unravel. He started drinking heavily and took up with the wanton wife of a cattle rustler. When the woman was arrested for carrying a gun, Hardin made the mistake of publicly haranguing and threatening the city's police chief, John Selman, once a dangerous outlaw himself.

That evening, as Hardin was rolling dice in the Acme Saloon, Selman came up behind him. According to Selman, Hardin spotted him in the mirror and went for his gun. Others claimed that Hardin was caught completely unaware. In any case, Selman shot him in the back of the head.

Four

The Kid

Men like Hardin, who lived by the gun, tended to die by it—usually at an early age. The average life expectancy for a Western gunman was about thirty-two years.

Billy the Kid barely made it into adulthood, yet he's been the subject of more books, articles, and movies than any other Western badman. Much of what's been written about him is based on speculation or legend.

No one knows for sure when or where he was born. In an 1880 census, Billy listed Missouri as his birthplace, and claimed he was twenty-five. But most historians believe he was born in New York City around 1859 or 1860. It seems certain that his given name was not Billy, but Henry. His father, an Irish immigrant named McCarty, apparently either died or ran off early on, because soon after the Civil War Henry's mother, Catherine, headed west with her two sons.

In Santa Fe, New Mexico Territory, she married a Civil War veteran named Antrim, and the family moved to the mining town of Silver City, where Catherine ran a boardinghouse while her husband prospected. Henry's life was relatively stable and uneventful—for a while. He attended school regularly and was, according to his teacher, "quite willing to help with chores around the

Though Billy the Kid was certainly no romantic hero, neither was he as cold-blooded a killer as this illustration implies. Note the anatomically impossible left hand.

schoolhouse." When the town put on a minstrel show, the future desperado could be seen on stage singing and dancing.

In 1874 his mother died of tuberculosis and Antrim, unable or unwilling to raise both boys, boarded Henry with the Truesdells, who owned the local hotel. Mrs. Truesdell remembered him as polite, hard working, and "the only kid who ever worked here who never stole anything"—until he fell in with a small-time thief known as Sombrero Jack.

In September 1875, the *Grant County Herald* reported that Henry had been arrested for stealing clothes from a Chinese laundry, but, the newspaper account added, "it is believed that Henry was simply the tool of Sombrero Jack who did the actual stealing." After sitting in jail for two days, Henry wormed his scrawny body up the chimney and escaped.

For two years he drifted, working first as a ranch hand then as a teamster at Camp Grant, an army post in Arizona Territory. Henry, still just seventeen, was generally called "the Kid." The post blacksmith, F. P. Cahill, was fond of tormenting the genial, likable Kid. He soon discovered that Henry could be pushed only so far.

According to an army scout, one day the burly blacksmith "threw the youth to the floor. Pinned his arms down with his knees and started slapping his face." Furious, Henry worked his pistol out of his waistband, pressed it to Cahill's ribs, and fired.

Cahill died the next day. Henry was locked up again, and again he escaped. Using the name Billy Bonney, he made his way to Lincoln County, New Mexico Territory, where he found work at the ranch of John Tunstall. Tunstall, a young, ambitious Englishman, quickly earned the Kid's admiration and loyalty.

Tunstall had taken the Kid on not as a ranch hand so much as a hired gun in a fierce battle to determine who would control Lincoln County. For years the most influential men had been Lawrence Murphy and J. J. Dolan, partners in a general store that monopolized trade in the county. Murphy and Dolan wanted no competition from Tunstall and his partner, lawyer Alexander McSween.

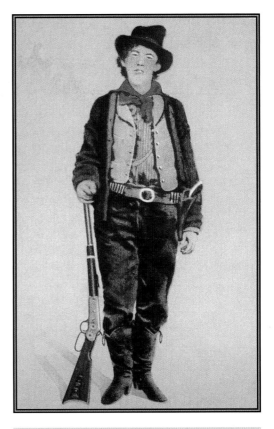

This photo, the only authenticated likeness of the Kid, has often been printed in reverse, giving rise to the mistaken notion that Billy was left-handed. In fact, a 1958 film about him is titled The Left-Handed Gun.

Claiming that McSween owed him money, Dolan tried to collect it by seizing Tunstall's livestock. As the Englishman was driving a band of horses, Dolan's hired guns overtook him and gunned him down.

The murder had a profound effect on the Kid. "I never expect to let up," he told a friend, "until I kill the

A Brief Encounter

Jesse James Meets Billy the Kid. It sounds like a low-budget Western movie from the 1950s. But there's evidence that the two most wanted men in America did, in fact, cross paths in the summer of 1879.

Jesse, on the run after the disastrous Northfield raid, had drifted into New Mexico Territory and put up at a hotel in Hot Springs. The Kid had just fled Lincoln County after being betrayed by Governor Wallace and may have been operating a gambling table in a neighboring town in the territory, Las Vegas.

Apparently Billy sometimes visited the hotel where Jesse was staying. On Sunday, July 7, 1879, he ran into two acquaintances there, a doctor and a former governor of New Mexico Territory. Both men recalled in their memoirs how the Kid introduced them to his new friend, "Mr. Howard from Tennessee." Billy later revealed to the two men that "Mr. Howard" was in fact Jesse James. Unfortunately, neither witness recorded the conversation that passed between the two outlaws, which must have been interesting. In December 1879, the *Las Vegas Daily Optic* reported that "Jesse James was a guest at . . . Hot Springs from July 26th to 29th. Of course it was not generally known."

last man who helped to kill Tunstall, or die myself in the act." He and other Tunstall men, as part of a posse called the Regulators, captured two of the killers. The prisoners never made it to trial; they were riddled with bullets, supposedly while trying to escape.

Three weeks later the Regulators ambushed Sheriff Brady and his deputy, who were allies of Murphy and Dolan. Dolan's men in turn killed Alexander McSween. The feud, known as the Lincoln County War, became such a scandal that President Rutherford B. Hayes removed the governor and replaced him with a former army general named Lew Wallace, better known as the author of the biblical epic *Ben-Hur.*

The Kid made the new governor an offer: He would testify against Dolan's men if Wallace would promise not to prosecute him for his role as one of the Regulators. Wallace agreed but, once the Kid had testified, refused to protect him. Though the Kid was in jail, he wasn't closely guarded. One evening he simply walked out and disappeared.

In the 1880 census the Kid listed his occupation as "one who works with cattle." Loosely speaking, that was true. Along with a small band of fellow fugitives, he had taken up cattle rustling. The gang worked out of Fort Sumner, a former army post in New Mexico Territory that had become a haven for outlaws.

The Kid was well liked by the residents, especially the local Mexican-American ladies. A friend described him as "a handsome youth with smooth face, wavy brown hair . . . and clear blue eyes. . . . Unless angry, he always seemed to have a pleasant expression with a ready smile. . . . His most noticeable characteristic [was] a slight projection of his two upper front teeth."

One of his casual acquaintances was a former buffalo hunter named Pat Garrett. In 1880 Garrett was elected sheriff of Lincoln County. At about the same time the Kid, whose criminal activity had consisted mostly of stealing horses and cattle, suddenly gained a reputation as the worst outlaw in the Southwest, thanks to a long article about him that appeared in the *New York Sun*. Its author coined the name by which he would be known forever after—Billy the Kid.

Pat Garrett couldn't ignore the growing demands for

the Kid's arrest. In December 1880 he tracked the Kid and his gang down to a deserted house near Fort Sumner and surrounded the place with a posse. "We could have stayed in the house," Billy said, "but . . . they would have starved us out. I thought it was better to come out and get a good square meal."

Movies and novels often portray Pat Garrett and the Kid as friends. Garrett did live for a year at Fort Sumner, and he and Billy undoubtedly met more than once. What's more, the lawman was married to the sister of Billy's girlfriend. But the two men were hardly close companions.

In April the kid was convicted of murdering Sheriff Brady. Since there was no jail in Lincoln, he was held in the court-house—ironically, the same building that had once housed the store owned by his enemies, Murphy and Dolan. One of his guards, Bob Olinger, who had fought on Dolan's side, took delight in taunting and bullying Billy.

Garrett cautioned his men that, given half a chance, the Kid would kill them "with as little compunction as he would kill a coyote." The warning proved useless. While Garrett was out of town and Olinger was at dinner, the Kid asked J. W. Bell to escort him to the privy. On the way back Billy apparently slipped one of his hands, which were unusually small, out of the cuffs.

There are several versions of what happened next. According to Pat Garrett, the Kid broke into the armory and grabbed a gun. Some historians suspect a pistol was hidden in the privy; others say the Kid seized Bell's weapon. In any case he shot Bell, then snatched up Olinger's shotgun. As Olinger came running to investigate, the Kid recalled, "I stuck the gun through the window and said, 'Look up, old boy, and see what you get.' Bob looked up, and I let him have both barrels."

Instead of fleeing the country the Kid went only as far as Fort Sumner.

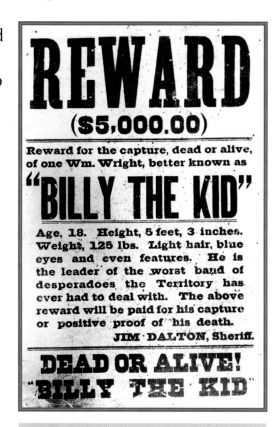

REWARD
($5,000.00)

Reward for the capture, dead or alive, of one Wm. Wright, better known as

"BILLY THE KID"

Age, 18. Height, 5 feet, 3 inches. Weight, 125 lbs. Light hair, blue eyes and even features. He is the leader of the worst band of desperadoes the Territory has ever had to deal with. The above reward will be paid for his capture or positive proof of his death.

JIM DALTON, Sheriff.

DEAD OR ALIVE!
"BILLY THE KID"

As this "wanted" poster suggests, the Kid used a variety of aliases. Two of his favorites were Kid Antrim and William H. Bonney.

Apparently confident that the law wouldn't pursue him there, he made little effort to conceal himself, even showing up at the weekly dances.

When Garrett learned this, he headed for Fort Sumner with two deputies. Around midnight the sheriff slipped into the house of a friend named Pete Maxwell, leaving his deputies on the porch.

A few minutes later Billy approached, meaning to carve a chunk from a side of beef that hung on the porch. Startled by seeing two men he didn't recognize, he drew his pistol and backed through the doorway, asking, "Pete, who are those fellows on the outside?" Then he spotted the shadowy figure of Garrett, sitting on the edge of Maxwell's bed. "*Quien es?* [Who is it?]" he whispered.

Garrett later wrote, "I drew my revolver and fired, threw my body to one side, and fired again. . . . The Kid fell dead. . . . He never spoke. A struggle or two, a little strangling sound as he gasped for breath, and the Kid was with his many victims."

Within a year of his death, no fewer than five mostly fictional "biographies" of Billy appeared. Even one coauthored by Pat Garrett was full of invention and inaccuracy. Myths about the Kid abounded, including the notion that he wasn't the man Garrett had shot, and the claim that Billy had murdered one man for each of his twenty-one years. The evidence suggests that he killed no more than five.

Five

The Poet

In 1875, the same year Billy the Kid "went to the bad," as a famous song puts it, a very different sort of outlaw was beginning a criminal career in the gold mining area of California. About all he had in common with the Kid was the fact that he worked under an assumed name: Black Bart.

He was born Charles E. Boles around 1829 in Norfolk County, England, and for the first forty-five years of his life showed no tendency at all toward out-lawry. His family emigrated to New York State when Charles was a year old. Soon after the gold rush began, he and his brother went to California to try their hand at prospecting.

His brother died there. Charles returned to New York, married, and took up homesteading in Illinois, where his wife, Mary, gave birth to two daughters. When the Civil War broke out, Charles joined the 116th Illinois Volunteers. According to records, he "served with great bravery." He marched through Georgia with General Sherman and was wounded in battle.

Boles came back from the war a changed man. Deserting his family, he drifted aimlessly around the Midwest and West for several years, finally ending up in

Because Black Bart held up only Wells Fargo stages, some speculated that he had a grudge against the express company. But the fact was, Wells Fargo had bought out most of its competitors, including the Overland Stage Company, so it would have been difficult to rob a stage that didn't belong to Wells Fargo.

California again. At first he made an honest living in the goldfields, but apparently not a very satisfactory one, for in 1875 he abruptly switched to the wrong side of the law.

Though the glory days of the rush were over, considerable amounts of gold were still being shipped out on the stagecoaches of Wells, Fargo and Company. In July 1875 a Wells Fargo coach was stopped near the town of Copperopolis by a tall figure wearing a duster—a long, lightweight linen overcoat—and carrying a double-barreled shotgun. His head was covered by a flour sack with eyeholes cut out, and two more flour sacks were bound around his feet.

"Please throw down the box," said the road agent in a deep, hollow voice. Over his shoulder he called, "If he dares to shoot, give him a solid volley, boys!" Seeing what looked like several rifle barrels poking from the brush, the driver quickly obliged. One of the passengers offered the outlaw her purse, but he refused it, saying, "Madam, I do not wish your money. In that respect I honor only the good office of Wells Fargo."

When a posse arrived, they discovered the smashed express box, minus $174 in gold notes. They also found that the "rifle barrels" were just whittled sticks. There was no point in pursuing the robber; his flour-sacked feet had left no tracks.

The masked man was, of course, Charles Boles. Over the next two years he robbed two more Wells Fargo stages. But it wasn't until August 1877 that he made a name for himself—literally. When the Sonoma County sheriff investigated the scene of a holdup, he found a poem, in several different styles of handwriting, on the back of a shipping bill:

> *I've labored long and hard for bread*
> *for honor and for riches*
> *But on my corns too long yove tred*
> *You fine haired Sons of Bitches.*
> *Black Bart*
> *the Po8*

Boles later revealed that he'd renamed himself after a character in a short story. Authorities felt the poem indicated that Bart had some special grudge against Wells Fargo—and he did, in fact, prey exclusively on that company's stages.

The following summer Black Bart struck again, and again left behind a bit of doggerel:

> here I lay me down to Sleep
> to wait the coming morrow
> perhaps success perhaps defeat
> And everlasting Sorrow—
> let come what will I'll try it on
> My condition can't be worse
> And if there's money in that Box
> Tis munny in my purse

It was the last such message the phantom poet would leave, but far from his last bow. Two months later there was a pair of Black Bart-style robberies near Ukiah. Indian trackers followed the bandit's trail for sixty miles over rugged terrain before losing it completely.

Wells Fargo detectives located a farmwife who had served a meal to their man. She described him as polite, comical, and intellectual, with graying hair and mustache, kindly blue eyes, and slender, "genteel" hands— in short, hardly the sort who goes around robbing stages.

Nevertheless, Boles pulled off sixteen more robberies over the next four years. None netted him more than $500. In November 1883 Boles returned to Copperopolis, the scene of his very first holdup. He later recalled thinking, "This was where I committed my first robbery. I

wonder if this will be my last!"
He was after a shipment of
amalgam—a mixture of silver
and mercury—worth more
than $4,000.

Though he followed his
usual procedure, this time
two things were different.
First, the strongbox was bolted
to the floor of the stage.
Second, the driver had an
armed companion, nineteen-
year-old Jimmy Rolleri. As the
stage started up a hill, Jimmy
jumped off and circled the hill
on foot, hoping to bag a deer.

At the crest of the hill
Black Bart stepped from the
brush. Following his orders,
the driver unhitched the team
and led them on down the
road, where he encountered
Jimmy. Borrowing the boy's
rifle, he fired twice at Boles,
who was chopping open the
strongbox with an axe. The
shots did nothing more than
alert Boles, who fled with the
money. "Here, let me shoot,"
said Jimmy. His shot nicked

*Charles "Black Bart" Boles was
such a respectable-looking fellow that a man who saw the
outlaw being taken in assumed
that Boles was the arresting
officer and that his companion—the actual detective—was
Black Bart.*

the retreating road agent on the hand. Boles stumbled, then ran on.

A search of the hilltop revealed a derby hat—which Boles probably wore under his flour sack to make himself look taller—some crackers and sugar, a belt, a magnifying glass, a razor, and a handful of buckshot wrapped in a bloody handkerchief.

The handkerchief proved to be Boles's undoing. In one corner of it were the letters "F.X.O.7"—a laundry mark that Wells Fargo agents traced to a man named C. E. Bolton. Bolton, who claimed to be in the mining business, was staying at a small hotel in San Francisco. According to his landlady, he was "an ideal tenant. So quiet, so respectable." In Bolton's room detectives found more laundry with the telltale mark, the famous linen duster, and a Bible inscribed to Charles E. Boles "by his wife as a New Year's gift."

When he was arrested, Boles indignantly proclaimed his innocence, but couldn't explain the wound on his hand. Eventually he gave in and led detectives to where he'd hidden the money from the strongbox.

Despite his confession he was sentenced to six years in San Quentin. From prison he wrote to Jimmy Rolleri, complimenting him on his marksmanship and assuring the boy he held no grudge. A model prisoner, Boles was released in January 1888 after serving just over four years. Now sixty, he was going deaf, and his eyesight was failing. To his abandoned family he wrote, "I am completely demoralized and feel like getting entirely out of reach of everybody." Though his wife offered to take him back, he advised her to "give me up forever."

Then he disappeared. For years afterward rumors abounded concerning his fate. In 1897 a Kansas man claimed to be Black Bart, but a Wells Fargo detective pronounced the man as much like the famous outlaw "as a bird's nest is like a mile post," and said that the original Black Bart had gone to Japan.

Others reported encountering Boles in the Klondike, in Panama, in Indian Territory. His wife's opinion was that "he is engaged in mining in some secluded spot in the mountains, though of course I do not know. He may be dead. God only knows."

Six

The Lady

In 1877, two years after Black Bart's first holdup, Wells, Fargo and Company compiled a list of known road agents. It contained more than two hundred names. Twenty years later, thanks to the arrival of the railroad, the stagecoach had become an outmoded form of transportation and stage robbery a thing of the past. But every era has its share of people who prefer to live in the past. Pearl Hart was one of them.

While Black Bart's reputation was based on twenty-eight robberies committed over a period of eight years, Pearl Hart achieved immortality by committing just one. It was notable for two reasons: it was the West's last stage robbery, and it was one of the very few holdups perpetrated by a woman.

Like most outlaws Pearl came from a respectable family. Born Pearl Taylor in 1871, she grew up in Lindsay, Ontario, Canada. In her teens she was sent off to a finishing school to learn how to be a lady. The lessons didn't quite have the desired effect. A slender, attractive girl with a quick wit, Pearl attracted a steady stream of admirers. But instead of bestowing her affections on just one suitor, she preferred to spread them around.

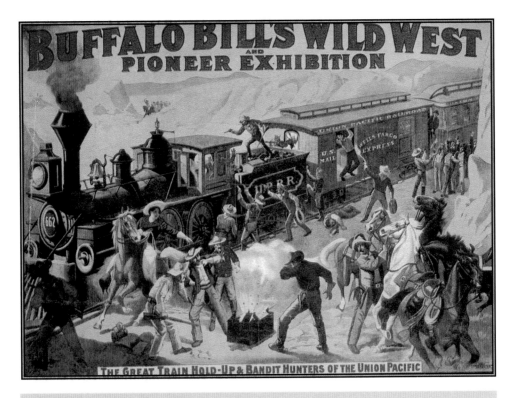

Colorful, carefully staged traveling shows such as the one managed by Buffalo Bill Cody gave impressionable Easterners a false, romantic notion of what the West was like.

When she finally did settle on one man, it was a poor choice. Frederick Hart was a small-time gambler and sometime bartender who had considerable charm but also had a pronounced lazy streak, a bad temper, and a drinking problem. At the age of seventeen Pearl ran off with him. In 1893 they settled for a time in Chicago, where Hart worked as a sideshow barker at the World's Columbian Exposition.

The Exposition's biggest attractions were the Wild West shows with their theatrical acts and mock battles between cowboys and Indians. Dazzled by this false picture of the frontier, Pearl deserted her shiftless husband, left her young son in the care of her mother, and headed west.

In Phoenix, Arizona Territory, she discovered that the way of life depicted in the Wild West shows no longer existed, if it ever had. She struggled to make a living by cooking and doing laundry for the local miners.

Then in 1895 Frederick Hart turned up, promising to mend his ways. He found a steady job as a hotel manager, Pearl gave birth to a daughter, and for three years they led a relatively peaceful and prosperous life. But eventually Hart slipped back into his old habits, and the couple began to quarrel. After a squabble in which he knocked his wife unconscious, Hart joined the army and went off to fight the Spanish in Cuba.

Pearl took her second child to her mother's home in Ontario, then returned to the Southwest. She drifted around from one mining camp to another, working as a cook, but found the solitary, rootless existence so depressing that she attempted suicide several times.

Things began to look more hopeful when she took up with a carefree miner called Joe Boot. They became partners in a short-lived freighting business, then tried their hands at mining, without much success.

Then Pearl received word that her mother was seriously ill and couldn't afford proper medical care. "That letter drove me crazy," she later wrote. "I had no money. I could get no money. . . . I believe I became temporarily insane."

During her first months in prison, Pearl Hart reveled in the role of lady bandit, frequently posing for photos armed to the teeth and dressed in men's attire.

She and Joe came up with a surefire money-making scheme: they would hold up the stagecoach that ran between the Arizona towns of Globe and Florence. Pearl disguised herself as a man, in a flannel shirt, jeans, and a white sombrero. With her slight build and smooth face she looked more like a young boy.

When the stage driver stopped to water his horses at Cave Spring, Pearl and Joe appeared with guns drawn. There was no valuable freight aboard, only three passengers who contributed a total of $421 plus a watch. Pearl, recalling tales of how good-natured and generous road agents traditionally were, returned a dollar to each of the passengers, "for grub and lodging."

Then she and Joe mounted up and rode off into the hills—where they promptly got lost. After wandering around for days they ended up on the highway not far from the scene of the holdup. Joe's weary horse fell into an irrigation ditch and nearly drowned. Soon afterward a sheriff's posse caught up with them and took them to the Florence jail.

The woman bandit caused such a sensation that the sheriff had to move Pearl to Tucson. She attracted even more attention there, especially after she and a fellow inmate broke out and fled to New Mexico Territory. They were quickly recaptured.

Just before her trial Pearl made a showy suicide attempt: she threw a clump of white powder into her mouth and collapsed on the floor of her cell. A doctor was rushed in. After a brief examination he said dryly, "No one ever killed themselves by swallowing talcum powder, Pearl."

When interviewed by reporters, she announced defiantly (and ungrammatically) that "I shall not consent to be tried under a law in which my sex had no voice in making," and urged other women to defy the law until they were given the right to vote.

Her claim that she had robbed the stage to get money for her mother's medical bills won her the sympathy of the general public—and of the jury, who voted to acquit her. Furious, the judge tried her again, on charges of stealing the stage driver's six-gun. The all male jury found her guilty, and she was sentenced to five years in Yuma Territorial Prison. Joe Boot was convicted of highway robbery and sent away for thirty years.

Since Pearl was Yuma's first female prisoner, a special cell had to be set up for her. The guards hung around it a good deal, causing "enthusiasm that was harmful to discipline." At first Pearl delighted in bragging about her exploits, but at some point she changed her tune and took to lecturing her fellow prisoners on the sinfulness of crime.

Convinced that she had reformed, the citizens of Arizona Territory petitioned for her release. In December 1902, after serving only half her time, Pearl went free. Her sister, who lived in Kansas City, Missouri, had written a melodramatic stage play about her titled *The Arizona Bandit,* and for a short while Pearl starred in it. Then she disappeared from the public eye, only to be thrust into it again briefly when she was arrested for buying stolen canned goods.

No one knows for sure what became of her after that. Some say she opened a cigar store in Kansas City and died there in 1925. Others believe she returned to Arizona, married a cowboy named Bywater, and lived out her last years as a law-abiding ranch wife who never spoke about her colorful criminal past.

Seven
The Last of the Badmen

Though the old, lawless West was fading fast by the time
Pearl Hart arrived in 1892, it wasn't quite dead yet. One
Western outlaw was just beginning a career that would
last well into the twentieth century and enable him to
boast on his deathbed that he had "robbed more banks
than any man in America."

It wasn't just an idle boast. Over a period of thirty
years Henry Starr pulled off more robberies than the
James gang and the Dalton gang combined. Yet in all that
time he killed only one man.

Henry was born in 1873, near Fort Gibson, in what
is now Oklahoma but was then called Indian Territory.
The Starr family, members of the Cherokee Nation, could
claim several outlaws already, including Henry's uncle
Sam and his wife, the notorious "bandit queen" Belle
Starr. But then Indian Territory was full of outlaws,
many of them white men who had fled there to escape
the law. Henry later wrote that "my surroundings, the
very air I breathed, whispered of deeds of daring and
peril."

He attended school for three years, but then his
father's poor health forced him to drop out and work the

Belle Starr was notorious not so much for the crimes she committed, which were few and relatively minor, as for the criminals she consorted with, including the Younger Brothers and the Indian outlaw Blue Duck, pictured here.

family farm. When Henry was thirteen his father died, and his mother married a white man, C. N. Walker. Henry was certain that his stepfather, "a greedy rascal," was only after the family's land. When life at home became unbearable, Henry took a job herding cows at a ranch near Nowata.

One day a friend asked Henry to deliver a suitcase to town for him. A few miles down the road deputies stopped him and opened the case, to reveal two pints of whiskey. Selling liquor in the Territory was a federal offense. Henry was persuaded to plead guilty, and fined $100. "Though my friends all knew I was innocent," he wrote, "it did not remove the reflection from my character. I was lowered and cheapened in my own estimation . . . and I was only a kid."

By 1891 Henry was full grown, a handsome fellow with an athletic build, a dark complexion, and black hair and eyes. Unlike most cowboys, he "didn't use tobacco, coffee, or liquor, and was very proud of that fact." He tried hard to stay honest, but was unjustly accused again, this time of stealing a horse. Despite Henry's protests that the animal was a stray, he was taken off to jail in Fort Smith, Arkansas. Though he was acquitted, he wrote that "my heart was bitter with disgrace and my brain surged and throbbed with thoughts and desires of revenge."

In July 1892, he and two accomplices robbed the railroad depot at Nowata. Fleeing across the dark prairie, Henry rode headlong into a barbed-wire fence, leaving him "cut and bruised most outrageously." To add insult

Though Henry Starr enjoyed robbing banks, he disliked violence. More than once he got the drop on lawmen who were pursuing him, but declined to "put them out of the running."

to injury, the horse ran off. Authorities identified the saddle, and Henry was arrested yet again.

When he was released on bail, he decided to "scoot to the brush." A $1200 reward was offered for his capture. A former deputy marshal named Floyd Wilson caught up with Starr at Wolf Creek, near Nowata, and fired a warning shot over the head of the outlaw, who fired back. Wilson sank to the ground. Starr approached and shot the man again, through the heart.

The shooting didn't bother his conscience, Starr said, because it was a clear case of self-defense. Yet he was shaken by it and fled "like a frightened coyote . . . fear tugging at my heart." The killing of Wilson set off the largest manhunt ever mounted in the Territory for a single outlaw. Twenty deputies dubbed "the Starr militia" combed the Cherokee and Osage Nations, but Starr easily eluded them with the help of his neighbors, most of whom sympathized with him.

Many newspapers, however, denounced him as a ruthless desperado. Feeling he might as well live up to the image, Starr rounded up several fellow fugitives and set about robbing stores and railroad depots. When a frightened two-year-old began to whimper during one holdup, her father reported that "Starr told her not to cry and assured her that he would not hurt her."

Such stories were overshadowed by those that portrayed Starr as a fierce, almost superhuman "bogy-man." Bullets, it was said, bounced harmlessly off him thanks to a steel breastplate he supposedly wore beneath his clothes. His swiftness and accuracy with a gun were legendary. One man reported seeing him bag a running coyote at a distance of more than six hundred yards. Tales like these made most lawmen less than eager to encounter him.

His reputation didn't frighten a pretty girl named May Morrison, who insisted on "believing the good in me and rejecting the bad." In March 1893, hoping for a haul large enough to let him marry May and leave the Territory, Starr led a raid on the bank at Caney, Kansas.

An alarm was raised but the townfolk, according to the Caney *Daily Chronicle*, "rushed hither and yon, everybody calling everybody else to do something and nobody doing anything. The robbers quietly got on their horses . . . and rode off."

Encouraged by his success, Starr proceeded to hold up a train. When his gang couldn't open the safe, they robbed the passengers instead. But, a Fort Smith newspaper reported, "nothing was taken from the ladies or any of the male passengers who had the appearance of being working men." Starr said he and his men took in "$6,000 and a consignment of unset diamonds and no one was hurt, although we did a lot of firing as a means of intimidation."

In June the gang held up a bank in Bentonville, Arkansas. This time the citizens weren't so disorganized. Half a dozen opened fire, forcing Starr and his men to use the bank tellers as shields. Though they got away with more than $11,000, it was a robbery Starr would come to regret.

With the Territory swarming with lawmen, Starr headed for California, taking May with him. They made the mistake of stopping in Colorado Springs "to replenish the lady's wardrobe." A man from Fort Smith, where Starr had been jailed two years before, recognized the outlaw and notified the police. As Starr sat down to dinner, he was seized from behind and was mortified to

According to a fellow outlaw, Starr "wanted to be a bandit on the order of Jesse James." In emulation of his hero, Henry held up a train and then made a point of taking only from those passengers he thought could afford it.

find that he, "the 'Bear-Cat' of a bunch of sure bad hombres—had been arrested, without a shot being fired, by five pot-bellied policemen!" May was taken into custody, too, and sent back home.

Starr was tried in Fort Smith before Judge Isaac Parker, widely known as the "hanging judge." After a long lecture in which he accused Starr of having "a heart void of social duty and a mind fatally bent on mischief," Parker sentenced him to hang for the murder of Floyd Wilson.

"I never batted an eye," said Starr. "I was young and foolish in the head." He was, in fact, only twenty years old at the time.

Isaac Parker was once the most powerful and feared judge in the country. But as time went by, the "hanging judge" turned into a bitter, burnt-out old man.

In jail he read books avidly, hoping it would help him earn an honest living if he managed to be released. When a fellow inmate, the notorious outlaw Cherokee Bill, obtained a pistol and began shooting up the place, Starr volunteered to go reason with him. Somehow he talked Bill into giving up his gun.

The Supreme Court granted Starr a new trial and, by the time it came around, the "hanging judge" had been replaced. Now charged with manslaughter and robbery, Starr was sentenced to fifteen years in prison. He was such a model prisoner that his mother convinced President Theodore Roosevelt to set her son free after he'd served only nine years.

Starr moved to Tulsa, Oklahoma Territory, married a schoolteacher who gave him a son they named Theodore Roosevelt, and generally led "an honest, upright life." Then he learned that authorities in Bentonville were asking to have him extradited to Arkansas to stand trial for the bank robbery there. Alarmed, Henry went on the run again.

He and one of his old pals robbed a bank in Tyro, Kansas, and, three months later, one in Amity, Colorado. Starr successfully hid out for a time, but when he revealed his whereabouts to a friend, the man turned him in to the law. He returned to prison, where he once again convinced everyone (except his wife, who divorced him) that he had reformed, and once again was given an early release.

He tried running a cafe, but his reputation scared customers away, so instead he ran off with another man's wife and went back to robbing banks. Between September 1914 and January 1915 Starr held up no fewer than fourteen. Between jobs he and his girlfriend hid out in the one place no one would think to look—a house in the heart of Tulsa, two blocks from the sheriff's house and four blocks from the mayor's.

Reveling in his reputation as the "greatest outlaw of them all," Starr decided to do something no other outlaw had done: rob two banks at once. In March 1915 he and six accomplices rode into Stroud, Oklahoma. One group entered the Stroud State Bank, the other the First National Bank.

As the outlaws were making their getaway, towns-people began firing on them. Seventeen-year-old Paul Curry grabbed a sawed-off rifle used for killing hogs and pulled off a shot. The slug shattered Starr's leg bone. "I don't mind getting shot," Starr said, as a doctor tended him. "But a kid with a hog gun—that hurts my pride!" Nevertheless he commended the boy for his courage.

This time Starr was put away for twenty-five years, but as usual his exemplary behavior won him a short-ened sentence. When he was freed in 1919, he returned to Tulsa, remarried, and became involved in the city's fledgling motion picture business. His first project was a silent film titled *A Debtor to the Law*, depicting the fateful robbery in Stroud, with Henry playing himself. His share of the profits amounted to $15,000, but the movie com-pany refused to pay up.

Deeply in debt, Starr recruited a new three-man gang. In February 1921 they drove a touring car to

Harrison, Arkansas, where they held up the People's National Bank. The bank's ex-president, who was inside the vault, retrieved a hidden rifle and shot Starr in the spine. The outlaw lived for four more days, long enough for his wife, his mother, and his son to reach his side and say their good-byes.

Just before his fatal trip to Arkansas, Henry paid a visit to his son. "Profit by my mistakes, Ted," he told the boy, "and always live your life in a clean, straight manner. . . . Once a fellow falls, it's hard to rise again."

GLOSSARY

Anderson, William (?–1864)   Confederate guerrilla leader whose indiscriminate killing and bizarre behavior—such as wearing a garland of Yankee scalps—earned him the nickname Bloody Bill.

Brown, John (1800–1859)   Fanatical abolitionist who led a famous 1859 raid on the federal arsenal at Harpers Ferry, Virginia. After Brown was convicted of treason and executed, many Northerners regarded him as a noble martyr.

Dalton gang   A ruthless band led by brothers Bob, Grat, and Emmett Dalton, who served as deputy marshals before turning to horse stealing and bank robbing. Four of the gang were shot down during a disastrous raid on Coffeyville, Kansas, in 1892.

Garrett, Pat (1850–1908)   Buffalo hunter, Texas Ranger, rancher, and sheriff of Lincoln County, New Mexico. Garrett's wife was the sister of one of Billy the Kid's sweethearts.

guerrilla   One of a group of unofficial soldiers who, rather than fighting as part of an organized army, harasses the enemy by means of small surprise attacks and ambushes.

Hickok, James Butler ("Wild Bill"; 1837–1876)   Famed Civil War scout, Indian fighter, and frontier marshal who later performed as a sharpshooter in Buffalo Bill's Wild West Show.

Indian Territory   The area to which Native Americans from all over the country were forced to relocate. At one time it included what are now the states of Oklahoma, Kansas, Nebraska, and the Dakotas, but by 1866 the Territory was reduced to the eastern half of Oklahoma.

Jayhawkers   Union sympathizers who terrorized proslavery residents of Kansas and Missouri before and during the Civil War. Their Confederate counterparts were known as bushwhackers.

morphine   A narcotic derivative of opium, used to dull pain and induce sleep.

Parker, Isaac Charles (1838–1896)   The federal judge responsible for administering justice in western Arkansas and Indian Territory. In his twenty years of service the "hanging judge" condemned one hundred sixty outlaws to death; of those, seventy-nine actually went to the gallows at Fort Smith.

Pinkerton National Detective Agency   A Chicago company founded in 1850 by Allan Pinkerton, an emigrant from Scotland, to investigate railroad freight theft.

San Quentin   A California prison built in 1852 on a peninsula in San Francisco Bay.

Sherman, William Tecumseh (1820–1891)   A Union general whose troops pillaged and burned their way through Georgia in 1864, during the infamous March to the Sea.

Starr, Belle (Myra Maybelle Shirley; 1848–1889)   Independent-minded woman whose reputation as "the bandit queen" was due less to her own crimes than to her relationships with male outlaws such as Cole Younger.

Sutter's Mill   A mill in the Sacramento Valley where gold was discovered in 1848, setting off the great California gold rush.

Wallace, Lewis (1827–1905)   Soldier, governor of New Mexico, and author of historical novels, including *Ben-Hur*, which was made into a popular movie in the 1950s.

Wells, Fargo and Company   An express company founded in 1852 that provided communications, transportation, and banking services to the Western frontier.

Wild West shows   Popular outdoor entertainments that featured such acts as trick riding, sharpshooting, and staged Indian attacks. The most famous was Buffalo Bill Cody's extravaganza, which performed all over the United States and in Europe for three decades.

World's Columbian Exposition   The United State's second world's fair, held in Chicago from May 1 to October 30, 1893.

Younger, Cole (1844–1916)   A Confederate guerrilla and one of the original members of the James gang, which later recruited his brothers Jim, John, and Bob.

TO LEARN MORE ABOUT OUTLAWS

Books—*Nonfiction*

Baldwin, Margaret and Pat O'Brien. *Wanted: Frank & Jesse James: The Real Story.* New York: Julian Messner, 1981.

A thorough and accurate account of the James boys' lives and careers from boyhood to Frank's final years.

Green, Carl R. and William R. Sanford. *Billy the Kid.* Hillside, NJ: Enslow, 1992.

Part of the Outlaws and Lawmen of the Wild West series, this biography of the Kid is brief and readable.

Wukovits, John. *Jesse James.* Philadelphia: Chelsea House, 1997.

This volume from the Legends of the West series is well written and accurate, with a good selection of period photos.

Yancey, Diane. *Desperadoes and Dynamite: Train Robbery in the United States.* New York: Franklin Watts, 1991.

A short survey of train robbers and their methods, and the efforts of the Pinkerton agency to bring them to justice.

Books—*Fiction*

Fleischman, Sid. *Bandit's Moon.* New York: Greenwillow, 1998.

An orphan in 1850s California runs off with the celebrated bandit Joaquin.

Roberts, Willo Davis. *Jo and the Bandit.* New York: Atheneum, 1992.

In post-Civil War Texas Jo Whitman becomes involved with a young, gentle bandit named Rufus.

On-line Information*

http://wellsfargo.com/about/stories/ch3
Information about the history of Wells, Fargo and Company, and about its five historical museums.

http://www.sptddog.com/sotp/gunfighters.html
Part of the Study Web, this extensive website has biographies and pictures of famous outlaws.

* *Websites change from time to time. For additional on-line information, check with the media specialist at your local library.*

Historic Sites and Museums

Fort Smith National Historic Site, 301 Parker Avenue, Fort Smith, AR 72902.

   Visitors can tour the courthouse of Judge Parker, the jail that housed such criminals as Cherokee Bill and Henry Starr, and the gallows. Exhibits and videos on outlaws and law enforcement officers of Indian Territory.

Jesse James Farm and Museum, 21216 James Farm Road, Kearney, MO 64060.

   Features "the world's largest display of James family artifacts" and an audiovisual history of Frank and Jesse.

Lincoln Courthouse Museum, Highway 380, P.O. Box 36, Lincoln, NM 88338.

   The original Murphy-Dolan store, and the building where Billy the Kid was jailed. Videos, exhibits.

BIBLIOGRAPHY

Editors, Time-Life Books. *The Gunfighters.* Alexandria, VA: Time-Life, 1974.

Elman, Robert. *Badmen of the West.* London: Ridge Press, 1974.

Horan, James D. *The Authentic Wild West: The Gunfighters.* New York: Crown, 1976.

———. *The Authentic Wild West: The Outlaws.* New York: Crown, 1977.

———. *Desperate Men: Revelations From the Sealed Pinkerton Files.* Garden City, NY: Doubleday, 1962.

Jackson, Joseph Henry. *Bad Company: The Story of California's Legendary and Actual Stage-Robbers, Bandits, Highwaymen and Outlaws from the Fifties to the Eighties.* Lincoln, NE: University of Nebraska, 1977.

May, Robin. *The Story of the Wild West.* London: Hamlyn, 1978.

Metz, Leon Claire. *The Shooters.* New York: Berkley, 1996.

Moody, Ralph. *Stagecoach West.* New York: Crowell, 1967.

Nash, Jay Robert. *Encyclopedia of World Crime.* Wilmette, IL: Crime Books, 1990.

Peterson, Barbara Tucker, and Louis Hart. "Billy the Kid's Great Escape," in *Wild West,* August 1998.

Settle, William A., Jr. *Jesse James Was His Name: or, Fact and Fiction Concerning the Careers of the Notorious James Brothers of Missouri.* Columbia, MO: University of Missouri Press, 1966.

Shirley, Glenn. *Last of the Real Badmen: Henry Starr.* Lincoln, NE: University of Nebraska, 1965.

Stiles, T. J., ed. *Warriors and Pioneers.* New York, Berkley, 1996.

Utley, Robert M. *Billy the Kid: A Short and Violent Life.* Lincoln, NE: University of Nebraska Press, 1989.

Walker, Dale L. *Legends and Lies: Great Mysteries of the American West.* New York: Forge, 1997.

Woody, Clara T., and Milton L. Schwartz. "Pearl Hart: First Known Female Stage Robber in Arizona Territory." Arizona Historical Society, 1977. Pearl Hart http://www.geocities.com/SouthBeach/Marina/2057/Pearl_Bywater.html

NOTES ON QUOTES

The quotations in this book are from the following sources:

Introduction
Page 6, "a daring, gallant": Jackson, *Bad Company: The Story of California's Legendary and Actual Stage-Robbers, Bandits, Highwaymen and Outlaws from the Fifties to the Eighties,* p. xvii.

Chapter One: The Mexican Bandit
Page 8, "native or natural-born": *Bad Company,* p. 249.
Page 10, "As I grew" and "spirit of hatred": Horan, *The Authentic Wild West: The Outlaws,* p. 198.
Page 11, "live off the world": *Bad Company,* p. 302.
Page 11, "endeavored to lead": *The Authentic Wild West: The Outlaws,* p. 199.
Page 14, "filled with ladies": *Bad Company,* pp. 317–318.
Page 14, "one unbroken record": *Bad Company,* p. 319.
Page 14, "I hope so": *Bad Company,* p. 323.

Chapter Two: The Ex-Guerrilla
Page 15, "the most renowned": Settle, *Jesse James Was His Name: or, Fact and Fiction Concerning the Careers of the Notorious James Brothers of Missouri,* p. 125.
Page 17, "For a beardless": Horan, *Desperate Men: Revelations From the Sealed*

Pinkerton Files, p. 42.
Page 19, "was identified as": *Jesse James Was His Name*, p. 40.
Page 20, "persons who were": *The Authentic Wild West: The Outlaws*, p. 60.
Page 23, "went to brush": *The Authentic Wild West: The Outlaws*, p. 97.

Chapter Three: The Gunman
Page 25, "I became a fugitive": Elman, *Badmen of the West*, p. 116.
Page 27, "but while he": *The Authentic Wild West: The Gunfighters*, pp. 162–163.
Page 27, "or die in the attempt": *The Authentic Wild West: The Gunfighters*, p. 171.
Page 29, "cheer her and": *The Authentic Wild West: The Gunfighters*, p. 180.
Page 30, "a thoroughly reformed gentleman": *The Authentic Wild West: The Gunfighters*, p. 184.

Chapter Four: The Kid
Page 31, "quite willing to help": Editors, Time-Life Books, *The Gunfighters*, p. 183.
Page 33, "the only kid": *The Gunfighters*, p. 183.
Page 33, "it is believed": Metz, *The Shooters*, p. 18.
Page 33, "threw the youth": *The Authentic Wild West: The Gunfighters*, p. 17.
Page 34, "I never expect": Stiles, *Warriors and Pioneers*, p. 270.
Page 35, "Jesse James was": *The Authentic Wild West: The Outlaws*, p. 80.
Page 36, "one who works": *The Shooters*, p. 12.
Page 36, "a handsome youth": Utley, *Billy the Kid: A Short and Violent Life*, p. 109.
Page 37, "we could have": *Billy the Kid*, p. 159.
Page 37, "with as little": Peterson, "Billy the Kid's Great Escape," p. 33.
Page 38, "I stuck the gun": "Billy the Kid's Great Escape," p. 29.
Page 39, "Pete, who are": *The Authentic Wild West: The Gunfighters*, p. 78.
Page 39, "*Quien es?*" and "I drew my revolver": *Warriors and Pioneers*, pp. 294–295.

Chapter Five: The Poet
Page 40, "served with great bravery": *Bad Company*, p. 188.
Page 42, "Please throw down" and "If he dares": *Legends and Lies:* p. 144.
Page 42, "Madam, I do not": Moody, *Stagecoach West*, p. 310.
Page 42, "I've labored long": May, *The Story of the Wild West*, p. 67.
Page 43, "here I lay": *The Story of the Wild West*, p. 67.
Page 43, "This was where": *Bad Company*, p. 173.
Page 44, "Here, let me shoot": *Bad Company*, p. 143.
Page 45, "an ideal tenant": *Legends and Lies*, p. 150.

Page 45, "by his wife": *Stagecoach West*, p. 318.
Page 45, "I am completely": *Bad Company*, p. 192.
Page 46, "give me up forever": *Bad Company*, p. 195.
Page 46, "as a bird's nest": *Bad Company*, p. 211.
Page 46, "he is engaged": *Legends and Lies*, p. 155.

Chapter Six: The Lady
Page 49, "That letter drove": Woody, "Pearl Hart: First Known Female Stage Robber in Arizona Territory," p. 2.
Page 51, "for grub and lodging": Nash, *Encyclopedia of World Crime*, p. 1468.
Page 51, "No one ever" and "I shall not consent": *Encyclopedia of World Crime*, p. 1469.
Page 52, "enthusiasm that was": "Pearl Hart," p. 3.

Chapter Seven: The Last of the Badmen
Page 53, "robbed more banks": Shirley, *Last of the Real Badmen: Henry Starr*, p. 191.
Page 53, "my surroundings": *Last of the Real Badmen*, p. 7.
Page 55, "a greedy rascal": *Last of the Real Badmen*, p. 12.
Page 55, "Though my friends": *Last of the Real Badmen*, p. 17.
Page 55, "didn't use tobacco": *Last of the Real Badmen*, pp. 18–19.
Page 55, "my heart was": *Last of the Real Badmen*, p. 23.
Page 55, "cut and bruised": *Last of the Real Badmen*, p. 25.
Page 56, "scoot to the brush": *Last of the Real Badmen*, p. 27.
Page 57, "like a frightened": *Last of the Real Badmen*, p. 34.
Page 57, "Starr told her": *Last of the Real Badmen*, p. 41.
Page 57, "believing the good": *Last of the Real Badmen*, p. 44.
Page 58, "rushed hither and yon": *Last of the Real Badmen*, p. 50.
Page 58, "nothing was taken": *Last of the Real Badmen*, p. 55.
Page 58, "$6,000 and a": *Last of the Real Badmen*, p. 58.
Page 58, "to replenish": *Last of the Real Badmen*, p. 67.
Page 59, "the 'Bear-Cat'": *Last of the Real Badmen*, p. 69.
Page 59, "a heart void": *Last of the Real Badmen*, p. 113.
Page 59, "I never batted": *Last of the Real Badmen*, p. 111.
Page 61, "an honest, upright life": *Last of the Real Badmen*, p. 147.
Page 62, "the greatest outlaw" and "I don't mind": *Last of the Real Badmen*, p. 171.
Page 63, "Profit by my mistakes": *Last of the Real Badmen*, p. 188.

INDEX

*Page numbers for illustrations are in **boldface***